THE PARENTING 5

The Parenting 5: Practical and Independent Little People

First Published by Toddler Education Services Pty Ltd
ourdomesticmontessori@gmail.com

Copyright © Ruth Barker 2013
The moral right of the author has been asserted.
All rights reserved.
Without limiting the rights under copyright reserved above, no part of the publication may be reproduced, stored in or transmitted, in any form or by means (electronic, mechanical, photocopying, recording or otherwise), without the prior written permission of both the copyright owner and the publisher of this book.

Text/cover design Georgina Collis, Inspiration Please
Photography Sarah Long, Longshot Images

Edition: 2nd
ISBN Print: 978-0-9923103-2-5
ISBN E book: 978-0-9923103-7-0
Order number: 90510
RC-RAEU

National Library of Australia

*These books are dedicated to all
the beautiful children that I have worked with
in the past 26 years. You have taught me all
that there is to be found in life.*

*In particular to:
Francis and Conor
Isabella
Anna
And all of the children from
Toddler Education Services (2001 to 2011)
and Montessori 1:1 to the current day.*

*In memory of my own mother
Olive Florence Sally Barker, who nurtured
me for the first ten years of my life.*

*And with love to my husband, Kevin Grover,
who encourages me to share all that I am.*

CONTENTS

About the Author — i

Foreword — v

Safety Note — ix

Introduction — 1

1. The Planned Environment — 3

2. Human Behaviour in the Environment — 7

3. Managing Behaviour in the Environment — 17

4. Practical Activity in the Environment — 23

5. Examples of Life Skills — 29

6. Adult Commitment List — 47

References and Recommended Reading — 51

ABOUT THE AUTHOR

Ruth Barker was raised on a remote wheat and sheep property in Western Australia. She knew she would work with children from a very early age, as she would 'teach' her toys in the shearing shed.

Ruth went to Swanleigh Boarding Hostel in Perth where she was a Sunday school teacher, before going on to Edith Cowan University to study a Degree in Social Science, majoring in Child Development and Family Studies with a minor study in Applied Science (Consumer).

She spent a number of years working with children in the United Kingdom where she fell in love with the ideas of Dr. Maria Montessori. Ruth returned to Australia to study a Diploma of Montessori Education (Preschool).

From 2001 to 2011 Ruth was the Directress of a small preschool program in Adelaide, South Australia. In 2012 she closed it to begin Montessori 1:1, a successful business working with toddlers and young children making the transition to school. She specialises in the one to one mode of engaging children and showing parents and carers how to prepare environments in the home and childcare setting.

Ruth's passion is in early literacy development and helping children with special needs.

She writes regularly on the Montessori 1:1 Facebook page and on the blog:
Our Domestic Montessori.
https://www.facebook.com/Montessori11
http://ourdomesticmontessori.blogspot.com.au/

Ruth has worked with hundreds of children in many applications over the past twenty-six years. Here are some of the testimonial statements:

"Ruth has a real gift for working with children and a passion to match."
N. Davis

"Ruth is calm, patient and delights in watching the children discover and learn for themselves. She guides them but allows them to teach themselves. She respects and loves them and that allows them to flourish, be encouraged and nurtured."
M. Rose

"This extraordinary educator facilitated some significant learning for my children. Ruth is a committed, creative and dedicated educator."
S. Habel

"A very innovative Montessori program that I will want to hear more about, as your environment and materials Ruth are just beautiful. I so admire what you are doing. You are inspiring!"
J. Bowman – Author, Montessori At Home!

The Parenting 5 books derive from prior studies, as well as vast personal work experience. Ruth has an avid interest in the philosophies of Dr Maria Montessori, the latest neurological research from the Centre on the Developing Child at Harvard University and from Psychologist, Jodie Benveniste. Many of the ideas from these three sources are used throughout.

FOREWORD

Welcome to The Parenting 5. Over many years parents and carers have asked for practical guidance in the home or childcare setting, preferably without the jargon that comes with early childhood philosophies and behaviour management theories. The Parenting 5 comprises of five books to support parents and carers in developing environments that will assist preschool children to reach potential. Each book offers the application of advice through simple words and photography.

The books consist of:

1. Practical and Independent Little People

2. Sensory Motor Play for Little People

3. Developing Language and Literacy

4. Developing the Mathematical Mind

5. The World Around Them

Experience throughout the early years lays the foundation for both neurological and physical wellbeing. An excellent early environment delivers readiness for life. Never again is there a period that is so influential on the make up of the human being.

"Children come into the world with unlimited potential for delight and immediately commence the awe inspiring task of self-construction. The prime matter for this great work they find in their environment."
Renilde Montessori. The Common Sense of Montessori Pedagogy.

"The first 6 yrs of life are when the majority of our brain architecture is formed. The exceptionally strong influence early experience on brain architecture makes the early years of life a period of great opportunity and great vulnerability. Critical aspects of brain architecture begin to be shaped before and after birth and many fundamental aspects of architecture are established well before a child enters school."
Centre on the Developing Child at Harvard University.

Young children have innate traits that allow development to occur without much influence from the parent or carer. Children draw information incessantly from their environment to build neural pathways. This is done through a need to be independent, to show attention and concentration, a desire for self motivated exploration, for perfection and to be creative, amongst other tendencies. All the adult need do is provide a prepared environment that allows this natural process to manifest.

Preschoolers require pursuits they can actively engage with their hands. The Parenting 5 books emphasise activity through life skills and sensory/motor experiences as the most important modes for early development.

Time spent in front of television or computers is shunned, as this does not build good brains or strong bodies!

Towards three and a half to four years there is a neurological shift towards abstraction and the ability to understand symbolism. Should the children show an interest, this is the time to begin numeracy and phonetics. A small component of screen time may be introduced, if so desired, as long as it is realistic and supports learning.

Human relationships based on a culture of common beliefs, values and clearly defined limits for behaviour, which are effectively demonstrated by all members of the family or group, are important to development too.

Please also note a strong emphasis on economics and promoting a sustainable environment throughout the books. The focus is with providing an environment on a budget and by using common household items rather than many expensive commercial toys to initiate activity.

Enjoy!

SAFETY NOTE

Every endeavour should be taken for children to be provided with a safe and healthy environment. Parents and carers are encouraged to supervise at all times.

Ruth Barker takes no responsibility for any unsafe practices as a result of the use of these books.

The books include the use of small parts as an aid to learning. A safe and healthy environment occurs when children are constantly watched and cared for.

INTRODUCTION

This book is a guide for parents and carers regarding how to encourage children with learning all they require to become self-sufficient and to be responsible for their actions.

This is paramount to healthy human development.

Practical and independent children have a solid neurological foundation for:

1. Attention and concentration

2. Self-discipline and self-regulation of their behaviour

3. Muscular and movement development, both gross (large) and fine (small)

4. Sensory learning through touch, vision, hearing, smell and taste

5. Language and communication skills

6. Cognition in the way they think and process information

7. Emotional development, especially confidence, self-esteem and a healthy self-concept for life

8. Social skills and respect for others

9. Success with later academic experiences

A lack of practical skills and independence, where the children rely on others to conduct their lives, can often lead to under development, social introversion and isolation. As a result the children develop into adults who are not able to manage their lives and are often challenged emotionally, leading to insecurity and a poor self-image.

Chapter 1
THE PLANNED ENVIRONMENT

The environment ought to be carefully prepared and represent realistic human life. This enables children to engage many life skills from the moment they are mobile and weaned from their mother. Items that are used for internal comfort are discouraged from this time, such as dummies and comforters, as these do not effectively promote independence.

Sound development is achieved in an environment where there is absolute safety and security, based on clearly defined daily routines. Children under the age of three and a half years are easier to manage when they know what to expect as the day progresses.

This need becomes less important as time goes by but remains beneficial as it allows for a low stress environment that is imperative to healthy neuron development.

The environment should contain small furniture and tools that are ordered and beautifully presented. An ordered environment is vital according to Gretchen Rubin in her book, 'Happier at Home' (2012).

She suggests it contributes to a culture of inner calm, peace and serenity, where the brain remains organised and never chaotic.

Order makes play and learning a joyful experience for those involved, leading to mastery over ones environment and increases self-control and overall happiness.

For example, if there are two sets of children, one group in an ordered room and one group in a chaotic room, there is often quite a marked difference in behaviour. Little people simply like order and are completely disinterested in chaos!

The storage of toys in a box is a further example. Toy boxes cause breakage and for pieces to go missing. How could a child effectively learn or be able to complete the activity when they cannot find its parts? This is rather disrespectful to the child. What is more, toys boxes do not allow for the parent or carer to show the children appropriate lessons in the use of the toys. Toys and activities are far better displayed in an ordered fashion where the children can heed the purpose. It is best to display only a few at a time and exchange them weekly with those that can be stored.

Rubin suggests:

• Be as simplistic as possible

• Make room for the things that are required at a particular developmental stage

• Abandon any activities no longer needed for development or those that are old or broken

• Make additions/purchases for what is needed at the given time rather than collecting

Finally, any life skills or activity in the prepared environment should be *both pertinent to development and stimulating to the child. This too is necessary for a solid neurological foundation.

*The Parenting 5 books Sensory Motor Play for Little People. Developing Language and Literacy, The Mathematical Mind and The World around provide further required information for developmentally appropriate and stimulating activity.

Chapter 2
HUMAN BEHAVIOUR IN THE ENVIRONMENT

While environmental preparation is crucial, so is the culture (beliefs and values) and the limits for behaviour desired in the environment. It is necessary for children to be aware of these and to know what is expected, accepted and disallowed. This is commonly known as 'freedom within limits'.

Psychologist, Jodie Benveniste writes about establishing beliefs, values and limits in her book, 'The Parent Manifesto' (2011).

Benveniste advises:

"It's about living by the values and beliefs you want to instil in your children, behaving the way you would like your kids to behave and being the kind of person you want your children to be." (2013)

Modelling is the key to establishing preferred behaviour in children, as they see the adult as the purveyor of the way things should be, thus it is important to 'practice what you preach'.

Each adult in the given setting should:

• Decide what the positive and negative behaviours in the current environment are and write them on two separate pages

• Decide what needs to be changed from the negative side

• Carefully acknowledge the beliefs, values and limits that may work to change the unwanted behaviours

The following list of ideas may assist:

Acceptance for others

Adventure

Assertiveness

Authenticity

Beauty in the environment or self

Care for self and others

Compassion

Challenging growth and learning

Connecting with others or community

Contributing

Conforming to rules

Courage

Creativity

Curiosity through exploration

Encouragement

Equality

Excitement for life

Fairness

Fitness

Flexibility in change

Friendliness

Fun

Forgiveness for behaviour

Generosity

Gratitude

Honesty and truth

Humour

Industriousness

Independence

Intimacy

Fairness

Kindness

Empathy

Love and affection

Order

Organisation

Patience

Persistence

Power

Leadership

Reciprocity in communication and life

Respect for self

Others and environment

Responsibility for actions

Safety and protection

Self awareness of ones and others thoughts

Self care

Improvement of self

Self control

Improving skills and supporting others

Write down statements that indicate how the new beliefs, values and limits may work as 'a call to action'.

For example:

I won't get cross when a drink is spilt, as I need to recognise that muscles are developing. I will prepare wipes for when (toddler) spills a drink and model the cleaning up.
or
I will not fuss over mess and accept the need for (child) to become creative. I will organise the painting area with all the tools required for wash up.
or
We respect the right to speak without interruption at home. We will wait patiently, remind the children to wait and use 'excuse me'.

Communicate and model the new plan throughout the day and before the behaviour will likely occur.

For example:

"Here are some wipes in case we have a spill. Watch how to use them"
or
"Lets go and get our new water bowl ready, before we paint together"

or

"If you want to say something, you say 'excuse me please first"

While setting, modelling and discussing the culture and limits pertaining to the environment are important, so is the way in which the members of the family or group respect each others attempt to communicate. Communication is two fold, firstly to verbalise well and secondly, to listen carefully. This is commonly known as 'reciprocal communication'.

Preschool children do not have the verbal skill to effectively describe what it is that they are feeling and as a result they show physical and emotional behaviour to extend their message. Consequentially this could be happy or sad, calm or angry, confident or fearful.

According to parenting coach and behaviour consultant, Sylvia Habel (2013):

"Human behaviour is a language in itself. Children are trying to tell you the parent (or carer) what they want and need so they can feel more connected, powerful, free, safer or engaged.

They are expressing to the parent or carer:
This is what I want you to know.
This is what I am trying to tell you to do.
This is what is important to me.

Helping children recognise and identify the emotion they are experiencing will help them manage their feelings in the longer term. Give them words that they can use to assist.

For example:

Are you feeling sad?
It looks like you're very proud of your picture.
Are you frustrated that you're not getting what you want?
Your voice is telling me you're cross and you want me to stop.
Are you scared because you don't understand what is happening?
Your face looks like you're thinking a lot about what I'm saying to you."

Respecting each other in a reciprocal way means that children should never be ignored. This does not give them any value as a human being and therefore, they don't develop much confidence over time. This flows on to low self-esteem and an unhealthy self-concept in adult-hood.

Ignorance of children can also be a deterrent to overall learning, especially when they use questions to understand their world. For example, when the brain changes from concrete to abstract around the third birthday, children ask 'why' a lot. Preschoolers do so to acquire all they need to grow intellectually and ignoring these questions by not listening or responding does not help with their potential development or their overall knowledge of the world around them.

Chapter 3
MANAGING BEHAVIOUR IN THE ENVIRONMENT

The following is a useful plan when engaging with children at home or in the childcare setting:

• Provide a functional continuous routine where the same actions occur daily (with some flexibility) such as having the same bath and bed routine.

• Provide a beautifully designed space with child size furniture and ordered tools and activities.

• Decide on the beliefs, values and limits for behaviour.

• 'Start as you mean to go on' by clearly defining those beliefs, values and limits.

• Expect that children should respect the limits all the time, where no means no.

• Remind the children what the limits are in periods of calm or before the behaviour may happen.

• Ensure effective reciprocal communication by giving

value to helping children express their needs and through listening carefully to them.

• Address the children at eye level by crouching low or sitting on a low chair (this is more respectful than lifting the children off their feet).

• Positively reinforce appropriate behaviour and ensure positive reinforcement occurs for what the children have done, rather than the product produced or the children themselves.

For example:

"The dishes are super shiny today and stacked so nicely"
or
"I like the way your wet pants are in the basket"
or
" Yellow and blue make green on your painting!"

Instead of:

"You are a good girl for doing the dishes"
or
"You are clever putting the pants in the basket"

or
"What have you painted?"

• Clearly remind the children in a nicely spoken but firm tone, when behaviour is inappropriate.

For example:

"I am sorry but I can't help you when you use a loud voice"
or
"Excuse me but throwing isn't how we put things away, lets try again"

• Accept negative emotions from the children as normal and if it is possible, discuss the scenario when all is calm.

• Use consequences sparingly and not for children under three and a half years of age, as their brain development is not advanced to understand this process.

• Consequences should not involve hurting or shaming children; removing the activity and time with the adult is consequence enough for the children under school age.

• Ensure that consequences match the developmental level and the situation that has occurred.

Examples of inappropriate consequences might be:

Sending a two year old into an abandoned space for not putting away an activity or spilling something
or
Yelling at a three year old for wetting their pants and punishing them

- In the event of a severe tantrum, be present to ensure that children are safe by removing any dangerous items from the vicinity and show ignorance to violence and screaming; the children will soon realise they will not receive a reaction and that tantrums serve very little purpose in getting their own way.

- Once the children have settled comfort them and discuss your feelings about the event and the expected beliefs, values and limits required, using simple and effective language.

For example:

"I understand you feel sad but hurting each other is not allowed"
or
"We use a small voice in our house even when we are angry"

• Look for support from another adult and remove ones self from the scenario if need be, as modelling ones own anger is not beneficial; if another adult is not available, remain present but take some personal time to the side and breathe deeply to relax.

Benveniste suggests AAA parenting to help the adult assess the situations they find themselves in:

Assess:

What was the situation?

Where does it occur?

Who does it happen with?

Why did it happen?

Is there a pattern?

What therefore might be the cause?

How did we all feel at the time?

Aim:

What do I now think about this?

How can I change it to fit within my beliefs, values and limitations?

How can I change my own feelings and behaviour?

Were my reactions fair?

Am I being appropriate to developmental stage?

What can we all learn?

What do I need to instil in the child?

Act:

What is the summary of my new plan based on my beliefs, values and limitations?

How do I put the plan in place?

What was the outcome or do I need to change it again? What has the child learned?

Chapter 4
PRACTICAL ACTIVITY IN THE ENVIRONMENT

There are many types of life skills that children can do in the home and childcare setting that will promote practical skills and independence. In the childcare setting it is imperative that the space resembles that of a home as much as possible.

Young children can capably tend to any environment that they play and learn in as soon as they are physically able. This builds happiness, self-discipline, self-esteem and a healthy self-concept. They should be encouraged to care for themselves and others in the environment, as well as learn proper manners from the earliest moment.

Life skills can materialise in the following areas of the home or childcare setting:

The play and learning areas

The kitchen

The laundry

The bathroom

The bedroom

The garden

How well the children manage these tasks in the environment relies on the way that the adult has previously prepared it and successfully demonstrated the skills involved.

The following are principles to assist in preparing and managing the environment to ensure success:

• *"A place for everything and everything in its place!"* Keep a routine and ordered environment where the children feel in control and secure with their attempts to learn new skills.

• Ensure the children have the right materials that are safe, child sized and realistic, to manage the task as a whole. For example, when laying out a kitchen activity for cooking, ensure all of the ingredients and every tool required to manage the recipe are displayed. It is best to plan these types of activities in advance.

- Show an effective and reciprocal communication style at the children's level and ensure good eye contact is made.

- Demonstrate for the children a succinct, clear and accurate lesson for gaining the new life skills, including each tool required.

- Guide the children with the correct use of each tool and show them how to carry furniture, activities and any dangerous items, such as long broom handles and cutting implements.

- Begin with the most simplistic of tasks and build up to more advancing skills.

- *"Never do for a child what a child can do for themselves!"* Allow the children to always do anything they are able to do and that they want to do.

- It is vital for the adult to model the beliefs, values and limits created at all times. It is also important to model the manners that are expected using very clear speech and communication. This includes appropriate greetings and goodbyes.

• Allow the children to practise and repeat, without interruption to develop new life skills. Repetition is one of the main keys to skill success.

• Observe and follow the children's progress so that planning can be done to increase the level of skill.

• Use positive encouragement based on the process involved to carry out the activity rather than on the product being produced. For example, when working in the kitchen with children, concentrate on the processes of cooking (ie. cracking eggs, measuring items, blending) rather than the end production of the cake. It is the skills involved that give children the neurological and physical development that they require.

• Personal praise (such as *"good girl"*), negative words (for example, *"you don't do that"*) and constant consequences do little for long term personal development.

• Allow children to make errors and maintain a positive attitude during a spill or breakage. This respects their developmental stage. Condemnation does very little for long-term emotional development, where as, suggesting they try again to succeed shows them that they are encouraged.

- Give choices as much as possible in everything that young children do. This means providing limited options but allowing them to make the final choice.

Chapter 5

EXAMPLES OF LIFE SKILLS

1. In the play and learning area:

Children can organise and clean their own play and learning space and put away their activities and books. The photograph below shows an ordered shelf of developmentally appropriate materials. It is easy for the children to maintain this order whilst they are playing.

Provide a cleaning centre so that the children can sweep the floors, dust, spray and wipe tables and manage spills and breakages (safety first). The photograph below shows a simple cleaning centre set up so that the children can take responsibility for their own environment and actions. Small instructions over time assist children with the task. Children can also water any plants and design with flowers in their space.

2. In the kitchen:

In the kitchen provide all the tools applicable to the stage of development in a low drawer. Include tools for cooking with adults, for food preparation, crockery and cutlery for laying out their space. In the photograph below is a low drawer of skill diverse tools as an example.

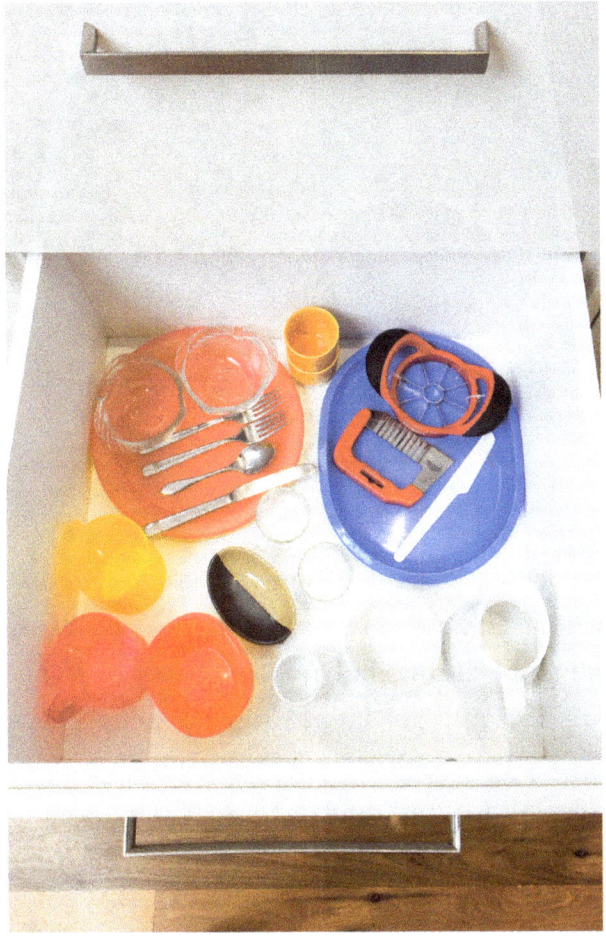

Provide a low-lying tray in the fridge and/or cupboard containing items for the preschooler to prepare their own snacks according to skill level. This gives them a great sense of independence and allows them to gain healthy eating habits for life with a nutritional selection available.

The preparation of simple food or exercises of cooking can also be done elsewhere in a kitchen tray, as well as lessons with the adult during daily food preparation. These exercises are not only pertinent to independent learning for life but they help to develop a young child's concentration and attention to a task and encourage the development of both gross and fine motor muscles and pre mathematical and literacy skills.

Examples are as follows:

• Using a ceramic jug and cups to practise pouring - The photographs below show a simple tray and then one with advancing skills through an increase in ceramic jug and cup size

- Using tongs and spoons to transfer items between dishes

• Using a knife for spreading onto bread or crackers

• Cutting with implements ranging from plastic through to metal, from blunt through to sharp

- Picking and collecting vegetable and fruit from the garden
- Scrubbing vegetables
- Peeling vegetables as shown in the photograph below

- Shelling peas
- Grating vegetables and fruit, cheese, cinnamon, ginger or garlic

- Making juice by hand or blender

- Using a melon balling spoon
- Making vegetable and fruit kebabs
- Sifting flour

- Cracking eggs/using a hand mixer and electric mixer

- Using a mortar and pestle (rock salt, egg shells or spices)
- Using a hand coffee grinder

Young children can set and clear the table, wash the dishes and load/unload the dishwasher.

They can also remove rubbish and learn about recycling from around three and a half years of age as shown below.

3. In the laundry:

Children can help to sort the clothes by colour and load them into the washing machine. They can also peg clothes and cloths to a small line or regular household air dryer. Another task is to care for pets by encouraging the feeding and cleaning of the pet's area.

4. In the bedroom:

The children will help to make their bed if they are provided with an easy set up. They can organise their clothes and dress themselves if they are given a simple system. Offer clothes and shoes at the children's level in baskets, on hangers or on hooks. It is often better to offer a limited selection of mix and match choices. They can pair socks and make attempts at folding.

Hanging coats can be done on low hooks and putting their shoes away near by.

5. In the bathroom:

Encouraging the children to manage their personal hygiene from around two years of age is pertinent to development. They ought to begin lessons in brushing, washing, dressing, toileting and putting their clothes in a laundry basket.

In the bathroom and toilet organise a range of tools that the children require to complete a task as a whole.

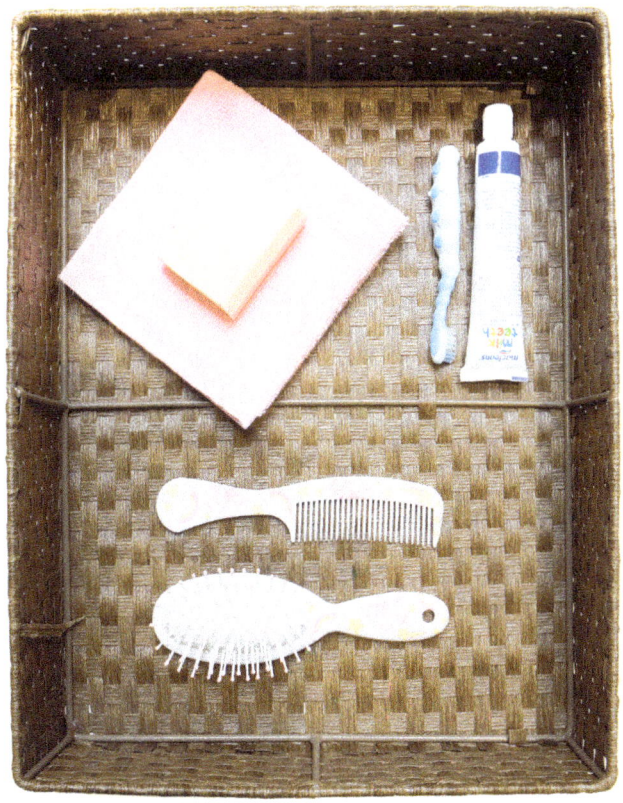

Provide a stool for the bathroom that can be used for washing, changing clothes and toileting, as well as baskets containing every tool required, including for fresh underwear and soiled underwear.

6. In the garden:
Children enjoy planting seeds, weeding, sweeping, raking and watering with child size tools.

Chapter 6

THE ADULT COMMITMENT LIST

Below is a list of suggested commitments that give application to the principles discussed in this book:

1. A safe and secure environment

2. A clearly defined routine that provides a predictable life style, especially in the early years

3. Child sized furnishings and tools that are ordered

4. Developing an environmental plan based on beliefs, values and limits

5. Model beliefs, values, limits and manners at all times

6. Expect the children to respect limits

7. Show effective reciprocal communication

8. Connect with the children at eye level

9. Show control over ones own emotions

10. Positive reinforcement before consequences that hurt or shame

11. Ensure any consequences are developmentally and situation appropriate

12. Accepting negative emotion as normal behaviour but ignore heightened tantrums

13. Discuss the beliefs, values, limits and emotions once the situation is calm

14. Prepare the environment for the child in all areas where they play and learn

15. Practical skills are pertinent to development

16. Practical skills are stimulating

17. Demonstrate the skills carefully with clear articulate language

18. Demonstrate the skills working with increasing difficulty as the children succeed

19. Remain calm during an error, spill or breakage

20. Give the children some choices in the things that they do, to encourage their independence

Preschool children that engage life skills in a well-designed space will have their developmental needs met and become practical and independent. As a result self esteem and a healthy self-concept will emerge and further assist their potential as a whole.

NOTES

Thank you for reading:
The Parenting 5
Practical and Independent Little People.

Also, look for:

The Parenting 5
Sensory Motor Play for Little People.
How to prepare learning activities to assist development and to prepare the children for academics.

The Parenting 5
Developing Language and Literacy.
How to communicate, activate both receptive and expressive language and develop the path to writing and reading.

The Parenting 5
The Mathematical Brain.
How to stimulate the early mathematical brain in numeracy, geometrics and early maths skills.

The Parenting 5
The World Around Them.
How to help the child understand the world that surrounds them through simple activity.

REFERENCES AND RECOMMENDED READING

The books and academic study of Dr Maria Montessori (1870 – 1952).

The President and Fellows of Harvard College. In Brief Series (2013).
Centre on the Developing Child. Harvard University.
• The Science of Early Childhood
• The Impact of Early Adversity on Brain Development
• Early Childhood Brain Effectiveness
• The Foundations of Life Long Health
• Early Childhood Mental Health
www.developingchild.harvard.edu

Benveniste, J. The Parent Manifesto (2011).
1st Ed. Parent Wellbeing.
http://www.parentwellbeing.com

Rubin, G. Happier at Home (2012).
Two Roads.
http://www.happiness-project.com/about/

Habel, S. Parenting Coach and Behaviour Consultant
President, William Glasser Institute of Australia
http://genleadership.com/

Sylvia recommends:
Buck, N. Peaceful Parenting (2002).
Black Forrest Press.

Ruth Barker has developed these books to support parents and carers to develop environments to assist children in reaching their potential. In doing so Ruth Barker has made all reasonable endeavours to ensure that the contents of these books are useful and accurate. There is no duty of care between Ruth Barker and the readers.

Under no circumstances will Ruth Barker be liable for any loss or damage, including but not limited to, direct, indirect or consequential losses, including any form of consequential loss such as third party loss, loss of profits, loss of revenue, loss of opportunity, pure economic loss and an increased operating cost, personal injury or death however sustained in connection with:
• The Reader's reliance on these books
• Any inaccurate or incorrect information presented by Ruth Barker or,
• Any act or omission (whether negligent or not) of Ruth Barker

Readers release and discharge and at all times will indemnify and keep indemnified Ruth Barker against any loss (including reasonable legal costs and expenses) claims, liabilities or expenses of any kinds, incurred or in connection with:
• Adverse consequences due to the Readers reliance on the materials in these books
• Any act or omission (whether negligent or not) of the Reader to any third parties/or
• Any damage, harm or violence caused by the Reader to any third parties.